ADELE'S JOURNEY

A true story of deliverance from sexual
immorality and the journey towards
righteousness

By

Adele Marie Newman

~ ACKNOWLEDGEMENTS ~

A very big thank you to my sons, Peter and Elijah for all your help. I love you guys!

In loving remembrance to my dear friend Beverly Colling who was instrumental in helping me get started with sharing my testimony. She is now awaiting the glorious resurrection! Hallelujah!

Heartfelt thanks to Charlie Garrett with the Superior Word in Sarasota, Florida. You are a dear brother, greatly appreciated and greatly loved!

A huge shout-out to my dear friend and brother in Christ, Michael Austin of PublishTheGoodNews.com! You are such a blessing.

To Joseph Arrington with Testimony4Jesus.org, words cannot express how grateful I am for the honor and privilege of counting you as one of my friends.

I wish it were possible to mention all those along the journey who have blessed and encouraged me to share my testimony. You know who you are. But, most importantly, the Lord knows who you are! Many thanks! I love you!

3

"Little children, these things write I unto you, that ye sin not. And if any sin, we have an advocate with the Father, Jesus Christ the righteous."

1 John 2:1

~ CONTENTS ~

~ INTRODUCTION ~

I recently heard of another famous Christian that "came out." Married for eight years with two young children, he struggled with same sex attraction since he was a teenager. He was raised in a conservative Christian home believing homosexuality was a sin. He suppressed his feelings and thought they would go away. But now he wants to be "true to himself" and "stop living a lie." He now believes this is what Jesus wants him to do and, is saying, he now has what the Bible calls "the peace that passes all understanding." Before coming out, he sought counsel from other Christians that have also embraced homosexuality. I don't know if he also sought counsel from those whom the Lord has delivered from homosexuality.

His story touched my heart. I can relate to what he said because I too walked in his shoes. Twenty-six years ago this young man's story was my story. Those who have not struggled with homosexuality just cannot understand. I know. I get it. I really do understand why folks believe they were born gay and there is nothing they can do to change. "Once gay – always gay." I used to believe that. For me, and for many others, it wasn't a "choice." I don't believe that most folks choose to have same sex attraction, nor to have gender identity issues. I used to believe I was a lesbian and that's how God made me.

I don't believe it is possible for anyone to change their same sex attractions. I don't believe it is possible for anyone to change their feelings or desires. However, I do know from personal experience that God can create in us a new heart with new desires. He can and will restore and renew all those seeking Him with all their heart. He transforms us according to His abundant mercy and grace. As we seek Him He strips away all that is not of Him. Feelings and desires are not sinful. *Acting* on sinful feelings and desires is. As we choose not to act on sinful feelings and desires, He starts working on taking away the desires. He creates in us a new heart! Some claim instant healing. For me it was gradual, over time, as I yielded to the Holy Spirit and chose to walk in obedience. I am now set free from homosexual feelings, tendencies and desires. Hallelujah! To God be the glory!

> *As the east is from the west, so far hath He removed our transgressions from us.*
>
> *Psalm 103:12*

I'm not alone in having this testimony. He's done it for me and He's done it for many others. By the grace of the Lord Jesus Christ He can do it for you, or your loved one. God is not a respecter of persons. *(Acts 10:34)* Praise God, great things He has done, is doing and will do!

It's not easy for me to write this book. I'd rather not pour out my heart in revealing very personal matters to complete strangers. But, I know it is past time to share my story. I cannot keep silent any longer. My love and understanding for all those either directly or indirectly involved in homosexuality compels me to speak out. I can no longer remain in my comfort zone.

Those struggling with same sex attraction or their gender identity need to know the truth. There are far too many voices out there trying to drown out the truth these days. It is absolutely possible to be completely set free from homosexuality, transgender identity issues and any other form of sexuality outside of God's plan for us.

I am not a hater of those in the gay community. Just the opposite! There are those still caught up in this lifestyle that I love dearly and continue to pray for. It is out of my love for this population that I am writing this book. I don't want anyone that is trapped in this great deception to suffer or perish. I pray with all my heart that the Lord will use me and my testimony to bring hope, encouragement and healing.

The following verse really spoke to my heart in regard to sharing my testimony:

When a righteous man doth
turn from his righteousness,
and commit iniquity, and I lay a
stumblingblock before him, he
shall die: because thou hast not
given him warning, he shall die
in his sin, and his righteousness
which he hath done shall not be
remembered; but his blood will
I require at thine hand.

Ezekiel 3:20

So, here I am, sounding the warning! There's no way I want anyone's blood on my hands!

This is my story . . .

CHAPTER 1

~ GROWING UP ~

My father was a good looking, smooth-talking, ladies man with lots of oats to sow. After marrying my mom and fathering four children, he decided to seek greener pastures with the secretary at his job. But, as Jeremiah 13:23 asks: can a leopard change its spots? I guess not this one! He found some greener pasture again. After fathering two children with his second wife, he left yet again for another woman. Not sure how many times he moved on but I do know I've got half siblings all over the United States. Hey, who knows, maybe the world? He was in the Navy and sailed to many ports. One never knows. I don't think he was a religious man but, it seems there was one Scripture he strongly believed in: be fruitful and multiply!

My father's leaving was a hard blow for my mom as her father did the same thing when she was a child. History repeated itself in her life. My grandfather cheated on my grandmother and left her for another woman. Because of this, my mom suffered greatly growing up. When my father left my mother, she had a complete breakdown and tried to commit suicide. I was three years old at the time. She was committed to the psych ward and my three siblings and I went into the New York foster care system. Those were difficult years, to say the least. We were bounced from one place to another. At first we were briefly all together, then my sister and I went to a girls' group home and my two brothers went to a boys' home. Then, I was placed in a home with one of my brothers. It switched up over the years but we were never all together again during the foster care years. We got to see each other and our mother the first Sunday of every month. I just couldn't wait for us all to be together as a loving family. For years I hoped for and dreamed of that day!

Well, that day finally came . . .

I was in the fifth grade when my mother married my stepfather and we were all reunited. Soon after, the loving family dream came to a screeching halt! My fantasy mother turned into a screaming, raging, crazy alien. This was *not* part of my dream! The first reality check was when she beat my younger sister with a can of furniture polish because she poured it on the furniture instead of the rag.

Right then and there, any dreams of us all living happily ever after quickly disappeared.

From that day on, I lived in great fear of her. Although she was released from the mental hospital, she was not healed from her mental health disability. She had a very violent temper that would flair up at anytime. She would fly into horrific rages that would completely terrorize me. She was depressed, angry and abusive - both physically and verbally. I used to hate her. I remember in one of her rages she stood at the kitchen sink screaming as she broke an entire set of dishes, one by one.

In 1975 I began my senior year in high school. A lot happened during that school year. My parents found out I had a black boyfriend and freaked out; cursing and screaming as they beat the crud out of me. He was my best friend. They didn't even know him but yet they hated him. I didn't understand why. Then, a friend of mine was killed in a horrible accident. I was so hurt and confused and crushed. Shortly after that my mother made another attempt at suicide and was put back into the psych ward. Nothing made sense. I couldn't understand why my friend, who wanted to live, was killed. Yet, my mother lived, but she wanted to die. Why? Why didn't God take her instead? I was reeling in so much pain with so many questions but no answers. I had always believed in God but now I had doubts He even existed.

In the late 1960's the "Jesus Movement" started and spread all across the globe into the late 1980's. It was during that time period that I got saved. This was an interesting time in history. During the sexual revolution of the 1960's with the rebellious counter culture movement, there was also a strong move of the Holy Spirit going on. It was amazing! Until the last few years, I have never seen anything like it. I do believe this is what is happening today. In this generation, along with the rampant growth of a wicked and perverse generation, there is a strong outpouring of the Holy Spirit. People are coming to the Lord in record numbers these days, especially in parts of the world where Christians are being persecuted and martyred for their faith.

Shortly after my friend died and my mother was committed, I stopped to listen to a street preacher talking about how to get saved. I believed in the Lord and wanted to be born again. I accepted the Lord Jesus Christ as my Savior. This was a few months before graduating from high school.

When my oldest brother turned 18, he got married and moved out. Then, a couple years later, when my second oldest brother turned 18, he got married and moved out. Then, a couple years later, when I turned 18 . . .

Yup, you got it!

I got married and moved out! Needless to say, none of our marriages lasted! *Hmmmmm . . . wonder why. . .*

A lot happened in my senior year. I was in the 12th grade when I turned 18 and got married, totally against my parents' wishes. Not that I cared about their wishes. They probably would have had better results if they pretended they *wanted* me to marry him. I think the only reason I graduated high school was because they claimed I wouldn't. But I was eighteen and could finally do what I wanted to do, and that was to get out of there! I was a tad bit rebellious and very strong willed, two survival skills that have both helped and hindered me over the years. I didn't realize it at the time but I just wanted a way out of all the madness. I wasn't prepared mentally, emotionally or spiritually for marriage. I had only known him a couple months. I wasn't in love. He was several years older than me and I mistakenly thought he had his act together. *Wrong!*

As a teenager I struggled with same sex attraction but thought it would go away. I didn't tell anyone. That was taboo in those days. I remember this horrible feeling shortly after we got married when I realized I had made a really *HUGE* mistake. I absolutely hated sex and would avoid it as much as possible.

I was serious about my commitment to receiving the Lord. I believed if I got a divorce, I would go to hell, so, I stayed for five years. I was completely miserable. He had issues. I had issues. It was a recipe for disaster.

A few months after getting married, I got pregnant with my first son. I was 19 years old when he was born. Two years later, my second son was born. I loved them both very much even though my marriage felt like a prison sentence. I felt completely trapped in a loveless marriage with no way out. I didn't read the Word back then. I didn't develop a prayer life or set aside time each day for the Lord. I wasn't fellowshipping with a Spirit-filled church. I didn't know it at the time, but, years later, I learned the church I was attending was classified as a cult.

After getting saved, there was no growth in my walk with the Lord. I remained a spiritual baby. It wasn't difficult to draw me away. The enemy knows all our weaknesses.

> *A sower went out to sow. . .*
> *some fell upon a rock; and as*
> *soon as it sprung up, it*
> *withered away, because it*
> *lacked moisture.*
> *Luke 8:5-6*

Five years into the marriage, I became friends with a co-worker. We really enjoyed each other's company. After working all day, we would spend almost all our off time either on the phone or doing stuff together. She even went to church with me. We became best friends. We felt completely safe to tell each other anything. Over time, our relationship grew into love.

This was the first time in my life that I felt truly loved and safe.

We were two "good" people that loved each other. We didn't want to hurt anyone. We just wanted to be together. It seemed so natural, so right. There was no question in either of our minds that we both wanted to spend the rest of our lives together in a loving and committed relationship. How could there be anything wrong with that?

> *There is a way which seemeth right unto a man, but the end thereof are the ways of death.*
>
> *Proverbs 14:12 and 16:25*

So, I decided to ask my husband for a divorce. I really didn't expect his response. After all, it wasn't like we had a loving, healthy marriage by any stretch of the imagination. I was hoping to calmly talk about the situation and that he would understand. Well, he didn't. He went completely off and flew into a violent rage! However, this wasn't the first time. He had a temper. I guess I should have known how he would react.

He said he wasn't that upset about me leaving him. What really infuriated him was that I was leaving him *for a woman*! He was angry because of the humiliation he would go through when people found out about it.

"What?!! Are you serious?!!"

He also said he heard rumors at the church about me and her but he didn't believe it.

"Really?!! Now that is outrageous!!!" I thought. We weren't even in a physical relationship at that time! If they were gonna gossip, they should have at least gotten it right!

Well, it got pretty ugly. He was threatening to kill both of us, so we moved out of the state, with my sons, and went into hiding. My sons were four and two years old at the time. They loved her and she loved them. We were all very happy together and I was planning to stay with her until death did us part; so to speak.

We worked separate shifts so one of us could be home with the boys while the other worked. A little over two years into our relationship, a male friend of ours started coming onto me. After he realized that wasn't working out for him, he switched gears. One night I came home from work and all her bags were packed. I said, "what's going on?!" Well, while I was at work, he'd come over and hammer her with how we were living in sin. A couple times, after throwing him out, I was able to convince her there was no way it could be sin if it was love. And, after all, God is love. She'd unpack and I thought that was the end of it.

But, no, he kept at it until she finally did leave. They got married. It felt like my entire world came crashing down. It was one of the lowest times in my life. I remember my oldest son and I sitting on the couch crying our eyes out.

After all those painful, lonely years, I finally had found someone who was really good to me and loved me. I was finally happy. How could love be bad? Why was God taking her away?

But I didn't know God back then. I didn't know how good He is or any of the great and wonderful things He had in store for me. I didn't know because I didn't read His Word - the Bible.

I was so devastated and confused. Was there even a God? If there really was and that was her reason for leaving, how could I compete with *Him*? There was no way. He's God!

The pain of her leaving was too unbearable. I didn't even want to live anymore. I was barely functioning.

But God!

My two most favorite words in the Bible: *But God!*

God knew if He was going to save us, it had to be her leaving – not me. I had no intentions of ever leaving her. He had to work in her heart first. He knew that I would one day come back to Him. Although it took many years to get over it, I can now say "Thank you Lord for your mercy, grace and long suffering."

. . . the riches of His goodness and forbearance and longsuffering; not knowing that the goodness of God leadeth thee to repentance?

Romans 2:4

CHAPTER 2

~ TIMES HAVE CHANGED ~

Years ago, when I was growing up, homosexuality was a dark secret that no one dared to let anyone know they struggled with. It wasn't talked about.

Prior to 1962, it was common practice in public schools to read from the Bible and to pray. Courts would not award custody to a gay parent. Gay couples were not allowed to provide foster care or to adopt children. My first lover and I used to tell people we were sisters because it was something you just didn't want others to know. It was shameful. The homosexual/bi-sexual/transgender lifestyles were things the majority of society did not accept, including those who weren't religious.

In May 1998 the very popular TV show "Ellen" was cancelled after she came out on air. She returned to television in 2001 but was unable to get strong ratings. It was cancelled after 13 episodes. Then the tide started to shift in the United States. She came back in September of 2003 and has consistently risen in the Nielsen ratings ever since.

Times really have changed. Now, public schools are prohibited from using the Bible, praying or even talking about Jesus. You cannot hand out Christian tracks on school grounds, even some college campuses. Children in public schools are now taught all about homosexuality and transgender lifestyles. Government offices and public schools are now required by law to provide gender neutral bathrooms and locker rooms or they will lose their federal funding. More and more businesses every day are following suit. It used to be a gay person was not allowed to serve in the military. On February 28, 1994, the Clinton Administration instituted "Don't Ask Don't Tell" for those serving in the military. Now, there are no holds barred for the openly gay serving in the US military, even to the extent of serious reprimand for "hate speech" to any speaking out in opposition. And, as most know, on June 26, 2015, the US Supreme Court declared same-sex marriages as legal unions in all 50 States.

The United States has fallen immensely in a short amount of time. The homosexual/transgender lifestyle is accepted as natural everywhere in our society these days. Just about anywhere we go in public these days, we will see gay couples blatantly displaying their affections towards each other. A huge change from the days when heterosexual married couples wouldn't dare to be demonstrative in public. We see it in TV programs, at the movies, in advertising, in mainstream media and news outlets, in workplace and school policies, on college campuses and even in a great majority of Christian churches. It is so easy to be confused and misled.

A professing Christian I know recently recommended a program for my son that a local Christian church sponsored. After looking up their beliefs I learned they were an "affirming" church that believed "sexual orientation, gender identity, or gender expression (or any other distinction) were not barriers, but blessings." They "welcomed all people into the full life and ministry" of the church. I didn't think she knew this so I cut and pasted their belief statement into an email to her. I was taken aback by the tongue lashing response I received on being a "true Christian." It stung. Then I had to stop and think of the world we are now living in. And, who is the god of this world?

> *In whom the god of this world*
> *hath blinded the minds of them*
> *which believe not, lest the light*
> *of the glorious gospel of Christ,*
> *who is the image of God,*
> *should shine unto them.*
>
> *2 Corinthians 4:4*

Every day I am getting to the point that nothing shocks or surprises me anymore.

It is becoming more and more difficult to stand up and speak the truth. Even some Christians do not want to hear what the Bible says. The world has gone past the point of demanding **tolerance** or **acceptance**. We are now living in the days that demand total **approval** of the homosexual, bisexual, transgender lifestyle. Those who voice their disapproval are targeted and punished. There is a growing hatred for those holding onto their Bible believing faith. There is no such thing anymore as freedom of speech or freedom of religion in our country. Conservative Christians are now being targeted for attacks just because of their beliefs. Your faith can now cost you your job, your business and even your life depending upon which part of the world you live in. Believers in other parts of the world are brutally tortured and murdered for their faith in Christ.

The cultural slide has been slow and steady in swallowing up the vast majority.

Not surprising. The truth is:

> *. . . wide is the gate, and broad is the way, that leadeth to destruction, and many there be which go in thereat.*

> *Matthew 7:13*

Although the world seems to be falling so far away from God, I am encouraged because I believe the Lord's return is drawing near. I know that everything that is going on here in the USA, the middle east and around the world are fulfillment of prophecies coming right out of the pages of the Bible. I believe we are living in the last days. There is no doubt we are now at a time in Biblical prophecy where many are being deceived by "the strong delusion."

For the mystery of iniquity doth already work . . . And for this cause God shall send them strong delusion, that they should believe a lie: that they all might be damned who believe not the truth but had pleasure in unrighteousness.

2 Thessalonians 2:7 & 11-12

CHAPTER 3

~ AN INCREDIBLE TESTIMONY ~

This is so awesome! I need to stop here and share my mother's incredible testimony.

After I got saved when I was 18 years old, I shared the Lord with my mom and she got saved. Shortly after she got saved, I received a call from her while I was at work. She was crying uncontrollably, telling me how sorry she was for all she did and begged for my forgiveness.

WOW! I couldn't believe my ears! *Who **was** this person?!!*

Well, I told her I forgave her but wasn't really feeling it. It wasn't until many years later after I repented and received the Lord's forgiveness that I was fully able to forgive her and then to love her.

From the time of her salvation until the day she died, about 20 years later, she kept growing and growing and being transformed. I praise God for that! I tell ya, there was no drug, no therapy, no psych ward on earth that could transform someone like that. That only comes from the

indwelling power of the Holy Spirit!
Hallelujah!!!

I wish I could say that was my testimony too.
But, I had a great falling away for many years
before turning back to the Lord. When I first
"came out" to my mother, she totally freaked out.
At first she didn't want to have anything to do
with me. At the time that was fine with me. We
didn't speak for a few years. Then, as she grew
in the Lord, she contacted me and we made
peace. Although she did not approve of my
relationships over the years, she decided to love
me and pray for me. Prayer is a very powerful
weapon, especially the prayers of a mother who
loves the Lord! I do believe her persistent and
fervent prayers played a huge part in my
restoration and healing.

Over the years, as her physical body slowly broke
down from the toll of diabetes, the Holy Spirit
kept growing stronger. First she had her foot
amputated. Then a below the knee amputation;
then the leg. Then the other leg. She had several
heart attacks. Then her kidneys stopped working
and she needed dialysis. She had it rough.
Really rough.

But in all that, His grace was sufficient for her!
Over time the Lord God completely healed and
delivered her from all the demons of mental
illness. It was amazing! She was at peace and
filled with hope. No more debilitating bouts of

depression, in-patient treatments, no more medications, no more shock treatments.

It was well with her soul. (I love that hymn!)

She found joy unspeakable – full of glory!

Through all the surgeries and long hospital stays in her later years she did not have a spirit of fear *"but of power, and of love, and of a **sound mind!"** (2 Timothy 1:7)* Glory to God! Great things He has done!

I am so thankful she got to see me delivered from homosexuality before she went home. Praise God! When she went home to be with the Lord in 1996, she was totally *NOT* the person she used to be! By His stripes she was healed. *(Isaiah 53:5b; 1 Peter 2:24)*

Now that's a testimony!

CHAPTER 4

~ FALLING AWAY ~

Shortly after my first lover left me, I got a job offer in North Carolina. We had been living in the deep south after my divorce. A total cultural shock for a New York born and raised Yankee but we won't go there. I decided to move to North Carolina. By that time it had been several years since my mother got saved and the Lord had been miraculously transforming her. Praise God! She and my stepfather offered to take in my boys until I found a place and got settled in. I packed a few suitcases to take on the Greyhound bus. All the rest of my furniture and stuff I put into storage. I had a friend at the time that was also moving. We decided to share a storage unit and split the cost. The plan was that I'd pay the first month storage fees and she'd pay the second. I did, she didn't. She never did pay the second month. She ended up splitting with all my stuff! Nice friend! With friends like that who needs enemies?!!

Well, I did end up getting a small place and a few months later got my boys back. I was able to function and hold down a job and support my kids but I was just going through the motions. I was angry and depressed and lonely and used drinking and getting high as an escape mechanism. All I wanted and all I kept searching for was to be loved. I was just searching in all the wrong places. I was angry with God. I went through a great falling away for many years before I turned my heart back to the Lord. I deeply regret all those wasted years in the wilderness.

> *The Lord is merciful and gracious, slow to anger, longsuffering to usward and plenteous in mercy.*
>
> *Psalm 103:8; 145:8; 86:15 & Joel 2:13*

How can we not love a God such as that?!! It just humbles me to tears.

He never gave up on me. What an awesome God!

After moving to North Carolina, I tried to finish college over the years but was never able to do so. That used to haunt me as one of many "failures" in life. Thankfully, I no longer measure success by the world's standards! God doesn't have the same measuring system as the world does. He has chosen the foolish things to confound the wise and the weak things to confound the mighty *(1 Corinthians 1:27)!*

Life was not easy being a single mom to two boys. I always struggled financially. I tried to get child support but their father dodged being served and that never happened. For many years I was angry and bitter about that. I hated him. Hate is like a cancer. It just festers and grows and nothing good comes from it. It only hurts the hater - not the person being hated. They're completely unaffected. By His grace, I no longer have hate in my heart. Praise God!

As the years went by, I became very involved in the gay community. That's how I identified. Although I was never satisfied in relationships, I kept searching. I kept trying to find what I had with my first lover, but I never did. I was very "out," bumper stickers, T-shirts, the whole nine yards. I went to rallies and marches for gay rights. One time I went with a bunch of friends to a march in Washington, DC. There was a gay newspaper back then called *The Front Page*. Well, there we all were: right on the front page of *The Front Page*! Yeah, I guess you could say I was a tad bit "out."

Although I had a lot of friends and we had an active life, I was not at peace and I was very lonely. There was an internal war raging inside of me. I loved my boys very much. I really regret messing up big time in raising them. I tried to be a good mom but I failed miserably. I wasn't equipped. I was too broken. I was in rebellion against the God who loved me and could make all things new. I didn't want to be gay. I tried over the years to be straight by sleeping with guys. It didn't work. I totally don't recommend that strategy! I'm ashamed to admit I was very promiscuous.

I was 34 years old when I became good friends with a guy I used to get high with. He was straight and I really liked him a lot. I even felt like I was falling in love with him. So, I told him so. Turns out he didn't feel the same way about me. So, what's the next best thing? His brother of course! Yes, I have to admit, I have made some seriously bad decisions in life. Really embarrassing to admit! Well, we dated for a couple weeks but it didn't work out. I wasn't feeling it. He knew I was gay, so no surprise for him.

It was during this time period that I could feel God working in my heart.

I was becoming so tired of running from God.

I started having this hunger and desire to get right with God. At that time, however, I didn't think there was anything wrong with being gay as long as there was a committed, monogamous relationship and not sleeping around. Thankfully, at the time, I wasn't in a relationship.

I started reading the Bible and going to church. My life finally seemed like it was on the right track. Or, so I thought.

A few weeks later . . .

the bottom fell out!

CHAPTER 5

~ THE DAY THE WORLD STOPPED SPINNING ~

I'm going to hit the "pause" button here and back up a few years.

When I was in my mid 20's, I became very ill and was rushed to the emergency room. Turns out I had an ectopic pregnancy. Meaning that the fertilized egg was stuck in one of my fallopian tubes. But the tube had burst. So they did emergency surgery. When I woke up, the doctors told me they sewed that tube up but discovered a bilateral dermoid tumor on the other tube and ovary. To remove the tumor they also had to remove that tube and ovary. Well, the good news was that I wouldn't be able to get pregnant. No problem there!

Right?!!

Wrong!!!

OK. . . hitting "play" again . . .

It turns out that somehow during that brief two week period of dating my friend's brother, I got pregnant!

What are the chances?!!! Taking into consideration there is only a small window in the month to ovulate. Plus, only having one ovary and one tube. And, that tube had been sewn up.

What are the chances of getting pregnant?

I'm going with: slim to none!

I was in complete shock! *Horrified* was more like it*!!!*

I was rushed in for an exam because the thought was that the fetus was stuck in that tube that had been sewn up. Which I was actually hoping was the case. That would be an easy fix to the problem without having to have an abortion.

So there I was, lying on the exam table getting an ultrasound to determine where exactly was this little "surprise." I was still in a state of shock and in no mood for cheery conversation. But lucky me got "Chatty Patty" as the technician! She was just jabbering away as she slid her little wand all over my jelly belly while looking at the computer screen. At least she was good at multi-tasking! I just wanted to get out of there.

It didn't take long for her to report: *"Oh! There it is – safely in the womb!"*

I didn't say anything. That was *not* good news!

She cheerfully continued her exploration and asked, "so, what do you want - a boy or a girl?"

I muttered: *"Neither!"*

This was just not happening.

I was almost done raising my two boys single handedly. They were fourteen and sixteen years old. I was single. I was so looking forward to traveling when they went off to college. Not another eighteen years as a single mom! Been there – done that. No thank you.

Well, then she got quiet as she kept looking at the screen and rolling around on my belly. After a few minutes she stopped and said she'd be right back. I was like, "ok."

Then she came back with another technician and the two of them continued the wand rolling quest while looking at the screen, neither saying a word. After a few minutes they stopped and said that they would be right back.

Well, that was a little weird but, I'm still like, "okaaaaaay." Not exactly sure what to think at this point.

Then they came back with some head honcho looking guy in a white jacket. He takes over the wand rolling expedition while looking at the screen. None of them saying anything. Then, he kinda gives them some sort of confirmation by going: "Ummm hmmmm. Ummmm hmmmm."

He asked me to get dressed; he wanted to speak with me. Then they all left the room.

OK, so now I'm like, *"WHAT?!! What is it?!! What is going on?!! Am I Sigourney Weaver carrying the alien child?!!"*

After what seemed like eternity, they finally came back in the room.

He stated that the fetus had the characteristics of Down syndrome; but, they needed to test the amniotic fluid to know for sure.

"Oh! Is that what they think?!" I was thinking. *"Well, there's no way. I have two perfectly normal kids. That's not possible!"* Not knowing hardly anything about Down syndrome at the time, I said; *"Sure, go ahead, do the test."*

About a week later I was at home when the phone rang. A very monotone woman said the results were in and they were positive.

Ya know, have you ever had that time when the world just stops spinning and you become completely numb? You can't think or talk? You're paralyzed?

I very slowly thought, "Okaaaaaaay. . . positive is good. . . negative is bad. . . "

So I blurted out, "I knew it wasn't Down
syndrome!"

Then she said, in a tone like; "Look you idiot!"
and very condescendingly, "Ma'am, the baby has
Down syndrome!"

That was it! My world came crashing down.

I lost it.

I dropped the phone.

I collapsed in tears.

CHAPTER 6

~ NOT AN OPTION ~

Abortion was not an option.

After turning my heart back to the Lord, I repented for many things I had done in the past and two abortions were among the sins. I repented with all my heart and was truly sorry for ending those precious lives. There was no way I would do that again.

His father didn't quite agree with me. He kept badgering me to have an abortion. Then one day when he started pressuring me about it, I came up with an idea. I told him I couldn't do it but, after the baby was born, I would give him the baby and he could kill it.

He looked horrified but I think he finally got it. He never asked me again to have an abortion. He also decided not to have anything to do with the child either. His loss.

This was a really difficult time in my life. I had just recommitted my life to the Lord and not at the point of totally knowing how to trust Him. Well, actually, I have to confess, I'm still working on that to this day! But, it does get a little easier as the years go by. Back then, I didn't face problems, I self medicated through them.

Now, there I was going through one of the biggest crises of my life and not able to use any of my coping techniques: I couldn't drink, couldn't smoke cigarettes, couldn't get high. All I could do was eat. . . and so, that's all I did.

I have always struggled my entire life with being overweight. Just prior to getting pregnant I worked real hard to drop 40 pounds and was finally feeling good about my weight. Then, during the pregnancy, I went from 120 pounds to almost 200. For a short person, that's a whole lot of poundage to be packing. This also did wonders for my already low self esteem.

I never did get back down to the 120 weight but, maybe one day . . . or not!

Yes, it was a tough time but I continued to read the Word and go to church. I can say for sure, God really is close to the broken hearted.

One day I was feeling really down and couldn't stop crying so I decided to take my Bible to the park. I sat down and, even though I really didn't feel like reading it, I flipped it open anyway.

Wiping away some tears, I couldn't believe what I was immediately drawn to! This verse:

> *You that goeth forth and*
> *weepeth, bearing precious seed,*
> *shall doubtless come again with*
> *rejoicing.*   *Psalm 126:6*

WOW! Can you believe it?!!

Yes, I have come again and again and again rejoicing over the past 24 years!

There have been many times over the years the Lord has used a verse from Scripture to pop out and speak directly to me. Sometimes I get a good chuckle when I see the Lord's sense of humor. For example, just recently.

I had been having *a lot* of tooth pain coming from under one of my back crowns. Turns out I had an infection in the root area. The dentist gave me antibiotics that helped reduce the pain considerably but, I had to decide my next step. I could do nothing and see if it just ends up going away altogether. I could have them pull the tooth. Or, I could have them remove the crown, do a root canal and then get a new crown. I quickly ruled out pulling the tooth as an option. I like to eat too much and I need all the choppers I have. Well, the cost is always the number one factor in all my decision making. The story of my life, but we won't go there. So, putting the

cost of a new crown on my credit card was scary.
I wasn't sure what to do.

This morning, as I sat down and flipped open my
Bible getting ready to find where I left off last,
my eyes fell on the following verse:

> *Thus saith the Lord God . . . take
> off the crown.*
>
> *Ezekiel 21:26*

I kid you not! Is that too funny or what?!!

I sure did get a good laugh. So, yes, the crown is
coming off!

God is so good. How can you not just want to be
under His wing?!!

I'm not going to go too much into how blessed
my life has been since giving birth to Elijah Luke.
I'm saving that for my next book! However,
what I will say is, God knew exactly what I
needed to pick me up out of the miry clay and set
my feet on solid ground!

> *For I know the thoughts that I
> think toward you, saith the
> Lord, thoughts of peace, and
> not of evil, to give you an
> expected end.*
>
> *Jeremiah 29:11*

CHAPTER 7

~ CLEAR TO ME ~

Shortly after turning my heart back to the Lord, I poured myself into reading the Bible. I soon found something very undeniable in the Word:

God hates homosexuality!

I remember this horrible feeling coming over me as I read the verses, over and over again. There was no getting around it. It was pretty clear to me.

Here's what the Bible has to say about homosexuality:

> *Thou shalt not lie with mankind as with womankind: it is an abomination.*
> *Leviticus 18:22*

> *If a man also lie with mankind, as he lieth with a woman both of them have committed an abomination: they shall surely be put to death; their blood shall be upon them.*
> *Leviticus 20:13*

*For this cause God gave them up unto **vile affections**: for even their women did change the natural use into that which is against nature. And likewise also the men, leaving the natural use of the woman, burned in their lust one toward another. God gave them over to a **reprobate mind** to do those things which are not convenient; Being filled with **all unrighteousness, fornication, wickedness . . . haters of God**,* *despiteful, proud, boasters, inventors of evil things . . . . covenant breakers* (divorce is just as high with Christians as non-believers). *Who, knowing the judgment of God, that they which commit such things are worthy of death, not only do the same, but have **pleasure in them that do them**.*

Romans 1:26-32

*Know ye not that the
unrighteous shall not inherit the
kingdom of God? Be not
deceived; neither fornicators,
nor idolaters, nor adulterers,
nor effeminate, nor abusers of
themselves with mankind.*
                    1 Corinthians 6:9

*Even as Sodom and Gomorrah,
and the cities about them in like
manner, giving themselves over
to fornication, and going after
unnatural lust, are set forth for
an example, suffering the
vengeance of eternal fire.*
                    Jude 1:7

That revelation brought me to my knees in tears.
I knew there was no way I could change what I
was or how I felt. As I was crying I kept
thinking: *"What am I going to do?!"* *"I'm gay!"*
"That is who I am."

I knew it wasn't me that God hated; just the sin.
But, I didn't know how to change who I was. It
was a terrible problem. I became overwhelmed
with this complete defeat to self. I just couldn't
do it. This total surrender to God came over me.
As I was crying my eyes out, I finally came to the
only possible conclusion:

"Lord, if you hate it, then You will have to change me. I just can't do it!"

As I look back over the years, I see many times in which the Lord created environments that seemed horrible at the time but turned out to be a blessing. Has that ever happened to you? I have learned to give thanks in all things. There is a lot I do not know nor do I understand. However, I have learned it is best to trust God in all things. His grace truly is sufficient for me! *(2 Corinthians 12:9)*

Well, the pregnancy and all the weight gain kinda took care of getting me out of the dating scene while the Lord began His restoration work in me. After giving birth I didn't have the desire to go "clubbing" anymore. I enjoyed spending time with this wonderful, adorable little surprise the Lord blessed me with. On one occasion when the baby was a few months old, a friend asked me to go to the beach for the weekend with her. There was some club down there she wanted to check out but didn't want to go by herself. I really didn't want to go but she was a pushy person. I told her I didn't want to leave the baby. She suggested bringing him and that the hotel would probably recommend a babysitter in the area. I was like; *"No way! I'm not going to leave my baby with a complete stranger!"* She couldn't understand and asked why not. I tried to explain that anything could happen; like, he could get kidnapped.

I was shocked when she replied; *"Do you **really** think someone would kidnap a baby with Down syndrome?!!"* Ouch! That hurt! She totally didn't get it!

Sad to say, her response kinda summed up the thought of lots of folks at that time. I heard of a 1994 study with pregnant women who learned the baby had Down syndrome. The results were that 97% of those women had an abortion. Not sure what the stats are these days. Oh . . . if only they knew . . .

God has used this unplanned and unwanted pregnancy to be my greatest blessing. Although, I didn't see it at the time. Life sure has not been easy over the years but I thank God every day for Elijah! God knows exactly what we need and when we need it. Oh, if we could only learn to give thanks to God in all circumstances!

As time went on, I continued steadfastly reading the Word and going to church. I learned from a study of the Word of God that He has not made *anyone* gay. He would not create someone to be something He hates. That doesn't even make sense. Think about it. God is good and loving and just and perfect. God did not make a mistake in assigning anyone the wrong gender. He's perfect! We were all created either male or female *(Genesis 1:27; Matthew 19:4; Mark 10:6).* We were given sexual desires to be satisfied through the sanctity of marriage to the opposite sex *(1 Corinthians 7:28; Hebrews 13:4).*

This is how we were created. When we live within the design of our creation, we have peace, satisfaction and fulfillment.

God is against *any* form of sexual immorality, not just homosexuality. Any sexual relationship outside of marriage is sin. Heterosexuals living together are living in sin. I know there are some who put homosexuality above all other forms of sexual immorality as if it were the unpardonable sin. *It's not!*

Here are some verses regarding sexual immorality in general:

> *But whoso committeth adultery with a woman lacketh understanding: he that doeth it destroyeth his own soul.*
>
> *Proverbs 6:32*

> *For this ye know, that no whoremonger, nor unclean person, nor covetous man, who is an idolater, hath any inheritance in the kingdom of Christ and of God.*
>
> *Ephesians 5:5*

. . . there should be mockers in
the last time, who should walk
after their own ungodly
lusts. These be they who
separate themselves, sensual,
having not the Spirit.

Jude 1:18 & 19

Behold, I will cast her into a
bed, and them that commit
adultery with her into great
*tribulation, **except they repent***
of their deeds.
Revelation 2:22

Please keep in mind, if you (or a loved one) are
struggling, having feelings is not a sin. We have
no control over what we feel. It is ***acting upon***
those feelings that becomes sinful. Everyone is
tempted and enticed. If we allow ourselves to
lust after the enticement then sin is conceived,
and, when sin is born, it brings forth death
(James 1:14-15).

The very first thing to do if you are being tempted
is ***RUN!!!***

*But thou oh man of God **flee***
these things. . .
1 Timothy 6:11

> ***Flee*** *also youthful lusts. . .*
>
> *2 Timothy 2:22*

> *. . .* ***Resist*** *the devil and he will*
> ***flee*** *from you.*
>
> *James 4:7b*

Hey, that's even better! Make him do the running!

If you are currently in a sinful relationship ***get out***! God cannot begin the restoration and healing as long as you continue in a sinful relationship. I really do know that it is not easy, believe me. We were never promised easy.

> *Whosoever will come after me,*
> *let him deny himself and take*
> *up his cross and follow me.*
>
> *Matthew 16:24*
> *Mark 8:34*
> *Luke 9:23*

> *They that are Christ's have*
> *crucified the flesh with the*
> *affections and lusts.*
>
> *Galatians 5:24*

Knowing this that our old man
is crucified with Him, that the
body of sin might be destroyed
that henceforth we should not
serve sin.

Romans 6:6

. . . he that suffered in the flesh
has ceased from sin that he
should no longer live the rest of
his time in the flesh to the lust
of men but to the will of God.

1 Peter 4:1 & 2

If you truly are a believer you have to make a choice: serve God or satisfy the flesh? You cannot serve two masters *(Matthew 6:24 & Luke 16:13).*

CHAPTER 8

~ DISCIPLES IN TRAINING ~

The Latin word "disciplina" means "training" or "discipline" in English. The Latin word "discipulus" means "a pupil" or a "disciple" when translated into English. Webster's Dictionary defines "discipline" as "self control, instruction, training of mind, body, or moral faculties."

Very interesting, huh?!

All believers in the Lord Jesus Christ are "disciples" and, as such, we are trained and "disciplined" out of the love the Father has for us. The same with parents that love their children; they discipline them. When a parent sees their little one getting ready to run across a busy street will they simply say, "Sure, go ahead!?" No! If they love their child, they would quickly grab him or her to keep them from danger or even death. Loving parents train and discipline their children to protect them from harming themselves along life's journey. Although the child is too young and inexperienced to know danger, the parent does. As the child grows he learns to trust that parent and to obey. Well, if that child is fortunate enough to have a loving, caring and unselfish parent that is. But, we'll go with the former for this illustration!

As believers, we have a loving Father who only wants the very best for us. He knows what we are up against and what the outcomes of our disobedience will be. He does everything to protect us, to nourish us and to help us grow up strong and victorious. Of course, we have that free will that keeps getting in the way. But, if we choose to trust Him and obey Him, we will be safe from harm and even eternal death. Ultimately, it is our choice to obey. We can't just satisfy every lust of the flesh. We must crucify the flesh. He sends us the Comforter to help us. Through the power of the Holy Spirit we can live in obedience. And, as we grow, as we deny the flesh, the Spirit grows in us and living a life pleasing to God becomes easier and easier!

It's a process . . . a journey . . . we are disciples in training!

It took time for the Lord to fully cleanse me of the attraction to the same sex. It wasn't over night, but He did completely create in me a new heart. That is what He promises to do! To God be the glory! And, if you are obedient, faithful and patient, He will for you too. He is not a respecter of persons *(Acts 10:34)*.

Always remember, you are not alone in this fight. You have many brothers and sisters who have gone before you in this same fight that can be strong encouragement to you. Above all, if you are a believer, you have the power of the Spirit of God that lives in you! Through the blood of Jesus there is a way out! You are an overcomer *(1 John 1:5)!* You can do all things through Christ Jesus who strengthens you *(Philippians 4:13)!* Allow the Holy Spirit to do what He promises to do. God is good and just and full of mercy. He would not call something an abomination and then not give a way out. He would not require something of us that we are unable to give or do.

The Lord himself goes before you and will be with you; He will never leave you nor forsake you. Do not be afraid; do not be discouraged.

Deuteronomy 31:8 NIV

. . . for He hath said, I will never leave thee, nor forsake thee.
Hebrews 13:5

Being confident of this very thing that He which has begun a good work in you will perform it until the day of Jesus Christ.
Philippians 1:6

It is very near and dear to the Lord's heart that we keep our bodies holy. Our bodies were created to be His temple for the Holy Spirit to dwell in us *(1 Corinthians 3:16)*.

> *Flee fornication. Every sin that a man doeth is without the body; but he that committeth fornication sinneth against his own body.*
> *1 Corinthians 6:18*

> *Know you not that your body is the temple of the Holy Ghost which is in you . . .*
> *1 Corinthians 6:19*

There is no real peace for a believer if they are living in sin. Paul talks about the constant struggle between the flesh and the Spirit in Romans 7:21-24.

> *For we wrestle not against flesh and blood, but against principalities, against powers, against the rulers of the darkness of this world, against spiritual wickedness in high places.*
> *Ephesians 6:12*

And, if there is no conviction, or no struggle . . . that's scary!

*Wherefore God also **gave them up** to uncleanness through the lusts of their own hearts, to dishonor their own bodies.*

Romans 1:24

*Now the Spirit speaks expressly that in latter times some shall depart from the faith, giving heed to seducing spirits and doctrines of devils. . . .**having their conscience seared**. . .*

1 Timothy 4:1 & 2

CHAPTER 9

~ STUDY TO SHOW YOURSELF
APPROVED ~

A huge problem is that many believers don't spend time in the Word. There are tons of books written *about* the Bible and, there are tons of daily devotionals out there. I'm not saying they are all bad. I actually love Our Daily Bread. What I am encouraging is daily reading and studying of just the Bible. This is our weapon of mass instruction on knowing God, all His warnings and all His promises. There is power in the Word! It is also very comforting. I have the Bible on CD. There are times when I am having trouble sleeping and it always puts me into a peaceful sleep.

I really encourage you to spend time daily in the Word. Delve into whole books in the Bible. Cross reference books and passages with other books and passages from the Old and New Testaments. If you don't have a Bible go to any used book store. All Gideon Bibles are free! How awesome is that?!!

Warning: it could seriously cut into some TV time!

The Lord does not want us to remain spiritual babies tossed to and fro and carried about with every wind of doctrine *(Ephesians 4:14).* Ignorance is not going to be an excuse on the last day!

*Seek ye out of the book of the Lord and **read**.*

Isaiah 35:16b

Study to show yourself approved unto God, a workman that needs not to be ashamed, rightly dividing the word of truth.

2 Timothy 2:15

. . .the Holy Scriptures are able to make thee wise. . .

2 Timothy 3:15

All Scripture is given by the inspiration of God, and is profitable for doctrine, for reproof, for correction, for instruction in righteousness, that the man of God may be perfect, thoroughly furnished unto all good works.

2 Timothy 3:16 & 17

I recently heard that approximately 50% of those claiming to be evangelical Christians do not believe there is anything wrong with being gay. Not surprising when many don't even believe the Bible is the Word of God.   Where does that put them?

> *Then He will declare unto them, "I never knew you, depart from me."*
>
> *Matthew 7:23*

I'm hoping and praying that the Lord will open eyes to see the truth in the lies that are being accepted in the body of Christ these days. It is my prayer that eyes will be opened to the truth and that the truth will set them free *(John 8:32)*. The Lord really has spoken to me over the years through reading the Bible.

> *For the word of God is quick, and powerful, and sharper than any two-edged sword, piercing even to the dividing asunder of soul and spirit, and of the joints and marrow, and is a discerner of the thoughts and intents of the heart.*
>
> *Hebrews 4:12*

What is going around these days about homosexuality and gender identity issues being okay with God are complete lies. Please don't just take my word about it, find out for yourself. Study what the Bible has to say about it. Be a Berean! It says in Acts 17:10-11 that the believers in Berea "received the word with all readiness of mind and searched the Scriptures daily to see whether those things were so."

I can accept knowing that those not saved have no problem with the gay lifestyle. If they aren't born again believers in the Lord Jesus Christ, it doesn't matter what they're into or even how good a life they live. They're lost. What really breaks my heart is when I hear of someone claiming to love the Lord Jesus yet accepting their homosexuality as how God created them. Or, when family members believe this is how their loved one was created.

There are two huge problems if you believe this:

1. You are deceived because you believe a lie that comes straight from the pit of hell; and
2. You will stop praying for deliverance and prayer is what changes things.

The truth is that God did not create anyone to have same sex attraction nor to suffer with gender identity issues. And, since this is not from God, He can and will take it completely away. Stand

on the Word of truth and rebuke the lies coming
from the pit of hell. Don't accept them.

If you are struggling with this great deception or
you have a loved one that is, don't stop praying!
Don't stop believing in God's promises. Answers
to some prayers don't happen overnight. The
Word tells us to always labor *fervently* in prayer
(Colossians 4:12).   Also, that the effectual
fervent prayer of a righteous man avails much
(James 5:15).

> *The Lord is good unto them that*
> *wait for Him, to the soul that*
> *seeketh Him.*
> *Lamentations 3:25*

Maybe you've been praying for a very long time
and there seems to be no change. What do you
do? Are you a believer? Don't stop believing!
That's where our faith steps in. It's easy to have
faith when we have instant results to prayer. But,
where is our faith when nothing seems to be
happening? In our fast food, high speed, instant
success culture we have grown accustomed to
getting it now. It's not easy for us to wait. Just
as our ways are not His ways, our timing is not
His timing. There is so much we don't know.
But, what we do know is that God is good. God
is patient and long suffering. He not only hears
every word we say but He knows our hearts. We
can trust Him. He will be true to His Word. No
matter how long it takes. It is our faith that

pleases God. It is our faith that breaks down the strongholds and crushes the lies of the enemy.

> *But without faith it is impossible to please Him* (God); *for he that cometh to God must **believe** that He is, and that He is a **rewarder** of them that **diligently** seek him.*

> *Hebrews 11:6*

No matter what the outward appearances look like - don't stop standing on the Word for complete deliverance and healing. There are many examples in the Bible of the Lord delaying in delivering what He promised. Abraham was childless when God told him he would be the father of many nations. He was an old man when God finally, many years later, gave him a son with his wife Sarah. And Sarah wasn't a spring chicken either! She was way past menopause when she finally got pregnant with Isaac.

God's Word promises healing and restoration to those who put their trust in Him. You can trust that God will do what He says He will do – in His time!

> *A new heart also will I give you . . . I will put my Spirit within you . . .*
> *Ezekiel 36:26 & 27*

*. . . I am the Lord that healeth
thee.*

Exodus 15:26

*O Lord my God, I cried unto
thee, and thou hast healed me.*

Psalm 30:2

If you are a born again believer in the Lord Jesus
Christ, you can lay hold of and claim all of God's
promises. They are faithful and true. God is not
a man that He should lie *(Numbers 23:19)!*

Spend time in His Word. Meditate upon it. Stay
in close fellowship with Bible believing
Christians. You are not alone in your struggle.
Here's some words of encouragement:

*And such were some of you:
but you were **washed**, but you
are **sanctified**, but you are
justified in the name of the
Lord Jesus, and **by the Spirit of
our God**.*

1 Corinthians 6:11

*I the Lord have called thee in
righteousness, and will hold
thine hand, and will keep thee.*

Isaiah 42:6a

*Remember ye not the former
things, neither consider the
things of old. Behold, I will do
a new thing.*

Isaiah 43:18 & 19a

*Therefore if anyone be in
Christ, he is a new creature;
old things are passed away;
behold, **all things** are become
new.*
2 Corinthians 5:17

Oh hallelujah!!! Amen!!!

CHAPTER 10

~ TROUBLE ON EVERY SIDE ~

We are troubled on every side,
yet not distressed;
we are perplexed, but not in
despair;
persecuted, but not forsaken;
cast down, but not destroyed.

2Corinthians 4:8 & 9

I was originally going to name this book "Adele's Testimony" but decided to change it to "Adele's Journey" because that seemed more appropriate. Our walk in the Lord is a ***journey*** in which we are ***being*** transformed *(Romans 12:2)* little by little as we grow from spiritual babes in Christ *(1 Peter 2:2)*. Like seeds that are planted in good soil need water to develop deep roots and grow, so we also must be watered to grow *(Matthew 13:3-8)* and *(Luke 8:5-8)*. Along the journey we will face lots and lots of temptations. That's just life. That's part of the growing process. One thing is for sure, never think that God is doing the tempting. God never tempts anyone *(James 1:13)*. Every believer is tempted and many have been tempted with the exact same temptation you are going through.

Suffering, persecution, struggles, stress, hard times . . .

Sound familiar? For the longest time, in my earlier walk with the Lord, I used to think if I was experiencing any or all of the above I had some spiritual flaw. I had this idea that those who are saved are "blessed and highly favored" and they prosper in everything they do, no suffering, no stress, no struggles, etc. By the way, this isn't exactly scriptural.

After repenting and turning back to the Lord I felt like I had this huge scarlet letter stamped on me. Going to church was difficult for me. I didn't exactly fit the "good Christian" outward appearance. I had recently come out of the gay lifestyle and still rough around the edges. I was a single mom, struggling financially with two teenage sons and a baby conceived out of wedlock.

I felt alone most of the time as I church-hopped trying to find a place where we belonged. The Lord used those days to teach me that things aren't always what they appear to be. I also have learned that it doesn't matter what others *think* of me. What really matters is what God *knows* of me!

Life was not easy. The Lord had a lot of work to do in me. There was a lot of pain and suffering.

Just as I am sure you have also experienced pain and suffering in your life.

The fact is, **ALL** that live Godly in Christ Jesus shall suffer persecution *(2 Timothy 3:12)*. Don't think it's strange *(1 Peter 4:12)*.

> *They were put to death by stoning; they were sawed in two; they were killed by the sword. They went about in sheepskins and goatskins, destitute, persecuted and mistreated . . .*
>
> *Hebrews 11:37 NIV*

> *Yes, and all who desire to live godly in Christ Jesus **will** suffer persecution*
> *2 Timothy 3:13*

> *We **must** through **many** tribulations enter the kingdom of God.*
> *Acts 14:22b*

Another thing we always need to be reminded of is that the enemy is not going to attack the unbeliever, the lukewarm believer or the believer living in sin. He's got them right where he wants them. He goes after those seeking the heart of God. He's like a roaring lion prowling around seeking whom he may devour *(1 Peter 5:8)*. He's a liar and a great deceiver. He is the father of lies *(John 8:44.)*

So, please be encouraged and hang in there! God is faithful! Although He allows stuff to happen, He will never allow us to be tempted above that we are able to overcome. Despite what you think and what you feel. And, He will ***always*** make a way to escape it *(1 Corinthians 10:13).*

Everyone makes mistakes. Everyone falls down. But, the faithful keep getting back up! *"A man falls seven times and rises up again" (Proverbs 24:16).* If we confess our sins He is faithful and just to forgive us our sins and to cleanse us from all unrighteousness *(1 John 1:9).* Be patient as you keep living for Christ and dying to self. Believe it or not, it does get easier!

> *For to **us** to live is Christ and to die is gain.*
>
> *Philippians 1:21*

Don't give up! Keep pressing on!

> *But this one thing I do, forgetting those things which are behind, I press on towards the mark for the prize of the high calling of God in Christ Jesus.*
>
> *Philippians 3:13-14*

We need to know how to fight the good fight and to win. To be victorious! To be more than conquerors *(Romans 8:37)!*

The only way to abstain from fleshly lusts that war against us *(1 Peter 2:11)* is by the power of the **Holy Spirit** who lives in us.

The only way that's going to happen is by our feeding, and getting nourished, and developing roots and growing! Numero uno: spending time in God's Word.

Numero dos: remembering to fellowship with the brethren *(Hebrews 10:25).*

He must increase and we must decrease along the *journey (John 3:30).*

CHAPTER 11

~ REDEEMING THE TIME ~

Because the time is very short!

Is your life busy? Do you often wish there were more hours in the day?

Well, let me tell ya, I *totally* get busy. I wrote the book on busy. Just kidding! Not yet. But, seriously, I do get it. Despite being a single mom for the past 38 years, struggling to make ends meet, I seemed to always be doing something in my "spare" time. Such as volunteering, new business ventures, various projects, you name it. Always running to and fro. A few years ago I began feeling like a hamster in a wheel just running and running and getting absolutely nowhere! If I had fifteen minutes to spend in the Word - that was good! I tell ya, there were lots of days I was just too busy to read the Word.

I really do believe Satan has been hard at work in the body of Christ keeping us very *busy* running to and fro! I see this in the lives of lots of folks I know and care about. I thought it would be a good idea to share a little on how the Lord spoke to me about this.

A lot of what I did was "good," but the Lord started opening the eyes of my understanding *(Ephesians 1:18)*. He showed me that not everything "good" is God. If I was too busy to read the Word, then I was too busy. If I was too busy to help a friend in need, I was too busy. If I was too busy to stop and share the gospel with someone, I was too busy. And, most of the time, I'm sorry to admit, I was too busy.

I took a long, hard look at my life to make some changes. I carefully examined my "commitments" to see what should stay and what should go. Some of my "busyness" the Lord took away from me.

I also had to learn how to walk away from toxic relationships that did not build up or edify my relationship with the Lord but rather were stumbling blocks. A huge waste of time and energy.

There's a difference in being "friendly with" and "being friends with." It's easier to get pulled down than to pull someone up.

> *Whosoever therefore will be a friend of the world is the enemy of God.*
>
> *James 4:4*

*Be ye not unequally yoked
together with unbelievers: for
what fellowship hath
righteousness with
unrighteousness? And what
communion hath light with
darkness?*

> *2 Corinthians 6:14*

*Bad company ruins good
morals.*

> *1 Corinthians 15:33*

*Behold, I send you forth as
sheep in the midst of wolves: be
ye therefore wise as serpents,
and harmless as doves.*

> *Matthew 10:16*

There have been times when, after lots of prayer,
I decided to distance myself from a professing
"Christian" friend because I was negatively
affected by our relationship. They were talkin'
the talk but not walkin' the walk. Do you know
what I mean? Have you ever heard the
expression: "Going to church makes you just
about as much a Christian as standing in a garage
makes you a car?" We can only tell a tree by its
fruits. Ultimately, only God knows the heart.

If someone's heart is not in the right place, there
is nothing (except prayer) we can do to change it.

God deals with matters of the heart through the Holy Spirit.

I'm a recovering people pleaser. My flesh wants to be friends with everyone. I don't want to offend anyone. However, in doing so, I realized I may be offending God.

I came across some strong words in the Bible about this type of situation.

> *Mark them which cause division and offenses contrary to the doctrine which you have learned and avoid them.*
>
> *Roman 16:17*

> *Now we command you, brethren, in the name of our Lord Jesus Christ, that ye withdraw yourselves from every brother that walks disorderly, and not after the tradition which he received of us.*
>
> *2 Thessalonians 3:6*

*It is reported commonly that
there is fornication among you .
. . deliver such a one unto Satan
for the destruction of the flesh,
that the spirit may be saved . . .
if any man that is called a
brother be a fornicator . . . with
such an one no not to eat. . .
Therefore put away from
among yourselves that wicked
person.*

1 Corinthians 5:1-13

*by their fruits you shall know
them.*

Matthew 7:16

It is so important for us to develop relationships
with other Bible-believing saints seeking after the
heart of God.

*. . . pursue righteousness, faith,
love and peace, **along with
those** who call on the Lord out
of a pure heart. . .*

2 Timothy 2:22

*not forsaking the **assembling of
ourselves together**, as the
manner of some is. . .*

Hebrews 10:25

81

*and they continued steadfastly
in the apostles' doctrine and
fellowship, and in breaking of
bread, and in prayers.*

Acts 2:42

*I myself also am persuaded of
you, my brethren, that you also
are full of goodness, filled with
all knowledge, **able also to
admonish one another**.*

Romans 15:14

*For the body is not one
member, but many.*

1 Corinthians 12:14

*Now you are the body of Christ,
and members in particular.*

1 Corinthians 12:27

We are living in a day and age in which the world
is under the strong delusion *(2 Thessalonians
2:11)*. Many are blinded to the truth and their
hearts have become hardened so that they cannot
see or understand and be converted and healed *(2
Corinthians 2:4) (John 12:40)*.

Some might ridicule and scoff at what I am saying in this book.

> *Knowing this first, that there shall come in the last days scoffers, walking after their own lusts,*
>
> > *2 Peter 3:3*

Some won't agree and may decide not to have anything to do with me. Such as one "friend" that refused to speak with me after reading a draft of this book. I get it. I understand. I'm OK with that. If God be for me, it doesn't matter who's against me.

> *For the time will come when they will not endure sound doctrine but after their own lust shall heap to themselves teachers. . .*
>
> > *2 Timothy 4:3-4*

Yes, we are in the last days . . .

*In the last days perilous times
shall come. Men shall be
lovers of their own selves. . .
blasphemers. . . without natural
affection . . .despisers of those
that are good. . . lovers of
pleasure more than lovers of
God; having the form of
Godliness but denying the
power thereof. . . led away with
diverse lusts. . . these also resist
the truth.*

2 Timothy 3:1-8

And . . .

*I cannot but speak the things
which I have seen and heard.*

Acts 4:20

Because . . .

*I am not ashamed of the gospel
of Christ: for it is the power of
God unto salvation to everyone
that believeth:*

Romans 1:16

CHAPTER 12

~ WHERE ARE YOU? ~

You've made it all the way through to the last chapter! Great! I do believe if you have gotten to this point, then the Lord probably is tugging at your heart strings. This is my closing chapter, but this is the most important chapter in the entire book. I pray you give it a lot of time and consideration.

Where exactly are you?

I have a few questions for you to think about.

> ➢ Do you know beyond a shadow of a doubt that if you were to die right now, where you would spend eternity?

> ➢ Do you know that all the promises, blessings, protections and healings that are given in the Bible only apply to the redeemed? Not to everyone.

> ➢ Do you know that we are *not* all children of God and that all religions *do not* serve the same God?

If you would, please stop and think about it for a minute or so. Maybe re-read the above three questions? It's important.

Yes, there is only one God.

> *Look to Me, and be saved, all*
> *you ends of the earth! For I am*
> *God, and there is no other.*
>
> Isaiah 45:22

Do you know that God loves you just as you are ~ right where you are? No pre-washing necessary!

> *I have loved you with an*
> *everlasting love; therefore with*
> *lovingkindness I have drawn*
> *you.*
>
> Jeremiah 31:3

There is absolutely nothing that God cannot forgive?

> *Who is a God like you,*
> ***pardoning iniquity*** *. . . because*
> *He delights in mercy.*
>
> Micah 7:18

*You have lovingly delivered my
soul from the pit of corruption,
for You have cast **all my sins**
behind Your back.*
Isaiah 38:17

*For You, Lord, are good, and
ready to forgive, and **abundant
in mercy** to all those who call
upon You*
Psalm 86:5

No matter what you've done, no matter where
you are, even if you are in prison reading this.

*To open the blind eyes, to bring
out the prisoners from the
prison, and them that sit in
darkness out of the prison
house.*
Isaiah 42:7

Just as there is only one true God, there is only
one way to God.

But He (Jesus) *was wounded
for our transgressions, He*
(Jesus) *was bruised for our
iniquities: the chastisement of
our peace was upon Him*
(Jesus)*; and with His* (Jesus)
stripes we are healed.
Isaiah 53:5

Jesus saith unto him, I am the way, the truth, and the life: no man cometh unto the Father, but by me.

John 14:6

Be it known unto you all. . . . by the name of Jesus Christ of Nazareth . . . neither is there salvation in any other: for there is none other name under heaven given among men whereby we must be saved.

Acts 4:10 – 12

For there is one God, and one mediator between God and men, the man Christ Jesus.

1 Timothy 2:5

Being justified freely by His grace through the redemption that is in Christ Jesus, whom God set forth to be a propitiation by His (Jesus') *blood, through faith.*

Romans 3:24, 25a

Who (Jesus) *gave Himself for*
us, that He (Jesus) *might*
redeem *us from all iniquity . . .*

Titus 2:14

Do you know that it is not God's will for ***anyone***
to be cast into the lake of fire?

The Lord is . . . longsuffering to
*us-ward, not willing that **any***
*should perish, but that **all***
should come to repentance.

2 Peter 3:9

And that He's coming back soon . . .

And now, little children, abide
in Him, that when He appears,
we may have confidence and
not be ashamed before Him at
His coming.

1 John 2:28

Therefore you also be ready,
for the Son of Man is coming at
an hour you do not expect.

Luke 12:40

Right now your salvation is nearer than it has ever been.

> *And that, knowing the time, that*
> *now it is high time to awake out*
> *of sleep: for now is our*
> *salvation nearer than when we*
> *believed. The night is far spent,*
> *the day is at hand: let us*
> *therefore cast off the works of*
> *darkness.*
> *Romans 13:11*

If you are not saved, or you are not sure if you are, call out to the Lord Jesus and commit your life into His hands!

> *. . .if you confess with your*
> *mouth the Lord Jesus and*
> *believe in your heart that God*
> *has raised Him from the dead,*
> *you will be saved.*
>
> *Romans 10:9*

> *Repent, and turn from all your*
> *transgressions, so that iniquity*
> *will not be your ruin.*
>
> *Ezekiel 18:30b*

If we confess our sins, He is faithful and just to forgive us our sins and to cleanse us from all unrighteousness.

1 John 1:9

Repent therefore and be converted, that your sins may be blotted out.

Acts 3:19b

God keeps His promises!

God is not a man that He should lie.

Numbers 23:19

Now unto Him that is able to keep you from falling, and to present you faultless before the presence of His glory with exceeding joy, to the only wise God our Saviour, be glory and majesty, dominion and power, both now and forever!

Jude 24 & 25

Thank you for taking the time to read this book. It is my heartfelt prayer that it has blessed you!

With love, In Christ, Adele

The grace of the Lord Jesus Christ, and the love of God, and the communion of the Holy Spirit be with you all!

2 Corinthians 13:14

NOTES